Elements of
Language
**First
Course**

Alternative Readings
Support for the Reading Workshops
Chapters 1–7

Introduction by Richard T. Vacca

- **MiniReads**
- **Teaching Notes**
- **Student Worksheets**
- **Answer Key**

HOLT, RINEHART AND WINSTON

A Harcourt Classroom Education Company

Austin · New York · Orlando · Atlanta · San Francisco · Boston · Dallas · Toronto · London

Table of Contents

**Use with the
Reading Workshops**

Table of Contents *(continued)*

MiniRead Summaries

Chapter 1: Reading an Eyewitness Account *(Pupil's Edition, page 18)*

"Going . . . Going . . . Gone!" *(page 4)*
This eyewitness account describes a fan's experience of watching baseball star Mark McGwire break a 37-year-old home-run record. Using descriptive language, the writer evokes the excitement of the crowd, the camaraderie of the players, and the specific action of the play. While the atmosphere of the exciting moment is an important idea in the MiniRead, the writer also implies that the good sportsmanship of Sammy Sosa, McGwire's friend and rival, was essential to the good feeling of the game.

Chapter 2: Reading Instructions *(Pupil's Edition, page 50)*

"The Crabmaster" *(page 9)*
These instructions for eating a crab are both informative and entertaining. The writer describes some animals' methods of eating crabs, then explains how humans should approach the task: with lots of newspapers for the mess and some tools for cracking the shells and extracting the meat.

Chapter 3: Reading an Advantages/Disadvantages Article *(Pupil's Edition, page 82)*

"To *e*, or Not to *e*" *(page 16)*
The writer discusses the pros and cons of using e-mail rather than other means of communication, such as letters and telephone calls. Among the advantages of e-mail are speed, multiple-copy capability, convenience, and ease of revision. Disadvantages include computer-related e-mail breakdowns, garbled messages, the number of people who don't have e-mail addresses, and the impersonal format. The writer concludes that although e-mail is useful, it is not always superior to older forms of communication.

Chapter 4: Reading a Novel's Book Jacket *(Pupil's Edition, page 118)*

"*Julie of the Wolves* Book Jacket" *(page 24)*
The MiniRead consists of a sample book jacket for the novel *Julie of the Wolves* by Jean Craighead George, including back-cover blurbs, a plot summary (not revealing the ending) on the front flap, and brief biographies of the author and illustrator on the back flap. The novel is about a thirteen-year-old Alaskan Eskimo girl who undertakes a harrowing journey to escape the traditional arranged marriage that her elders want for her. She gets lost, is rescued by a pack of wolves, and must choose between life with the wolves and life among people.

Chapter 5: Reading an Informative Article *(Pupil's Edition, page 158)*

"News from *Galileo*" *(page 32)*
The article describes the three major discoveries made by the spacecraft *Galileo,* which reached Jupiter in 1995. The first discovery is that Europa, one of the moons of Jupiter, contains liquid water. The second discovery is that there is heat, possibly created by the motion of tides, on Europa. The third discovery is that Europa may contain organic compounds. Liquid water, heat, and organic compounds are the conditions under which

MiniRead Summaries *(continued)*

life can develop. As far as we know, they have come together in only one other place—Earth.

Chapter 6: Reading a Persuasive Article *(Pupil's Edition, page 202)*

"Vanishing Species Vanish from Zoos" *(page 39)*
In this persuasive article, the writer discusses how some zoos overbreed endangered species to increase their numbers. Then, to handle zoo overcrowding, zoos sell surplus animals to game dealers. Dealers in turn may sell the animals to hunting ranches. The writer's point of view is that new laws and monitoring systems are needed to prevent these abuses. The writer uses a variety of logical support to argue in favor of laws that limit breeding and prohibit the sale of zoo animals to hunting ranches.

Chapter 7: Reading a Print Advertisement *(Pupil's Edition, page 234)*

"If You Really Care About Your Family . . ." *(page 46)*
This print advertisement uses persuasive techniques to suggest a potentially dangerous situation in which safety may depend on having a cellphone. The ad shows a broken-down car in the snow and says "Your kids are scared and freezing." The text of the ad targets the reader's fear of this situation as well as the reader's sense of responsibility to take preventative measures. The purpose of the ad is to persuade the reader to subscribe to "Super CellPhone SOS" for $39.95 a month.

About This Book

Introduction

Alternative Readings is an instructional resource designed to be used with *Elements of Language.* Teachers at both the middle school and high school levels have been asking textbook publishers to address the growing instructional need for materials that will help students who either lack fundamental reading skills or the motivation to retain and develop the skills they do have. *Alternative Readings* is a response to that need.

The Organization of *Alternative Readings*

The chapters in Part 1 of your *Elements of Language* Pupil's Edition each contain a **Reading Workshop.** Each chapter of *Alternative Readings* supports the Reading Workshop in the corresponding *Elements of Language* chapter. Chapters in this resource provide alternative lessons that teach the same reading skills covered in the Reading Workshops. The lessons allow struggling readers to practice and apply reading skills and strategies to short selections that are appropriate to their reading levels. The lessons consist of

- **Teaching Notes,** including **Alternative Strategies** for teaching nonfiction texts to struggling readers
- **MiniReads,** short, easy-to-read selections that feature the same mode of writing covered in the Reading Workshop
- **Alternative Strategy Practice Worksheets,** which help students apply the strategies and skills to the MiniReads

At the back of *Alternative Readings* you will find an **Answer Key** for the active-reading questions and worksheets in each chapter.

The Chapter Overviews

The Teaching Notes

The Teaching Notes begin with an Overview that briefly explains the reading skill that students will practice in the lesson and relates the skill to the mode of writing covered in the corresponding chapter of the Pupil's Edition. In the Overview you will find a list of the lesson contents, followed by a **MiniRead Summary** that describes the topic of the MiniRead.

Using the MiniRead

This section of the Teaching Notes contains *Before Reading, During Reading,* and *After Reading* suggestions for using the MiniRead and its accompanying **Active-Reading Questions.** If you choose not to use the Alternative Strategy, this section offers ideas for students to preview the MiniRead, activate their prior knowledge, and answer the questions that appear in the text.

About This Book *(continued)*

The Alternative Strategies

The second page of the Teaching Notes for each chapter contains the Alternative Strategy lesson. The Alternative Strategies are designed to help struggling readers develop and use the skills they need to read effectively.

- The introductory paragraph briefly explains the procedure students follow to apply the strategy to a text.
- **Modeling the Strategy** offers suggestions for *think-alouds* to model the strategy before students apply it to the MiniRead. This section guides you through modeling with a sample passage from the MiniRead or another short passage that is provided. Sample student and teacher comments are included.
- **Applying the Strategy.** This section highlights important points you might want to emphasize or clarify before students apply the strategy to the MiniRead using the **Alternative Strategy Practice** worksheet.
- In the margin you will find a list of **Strategy Options** that offer teaching suggestions and ideas for helping students who are having difficulty.
- **Extending the Strategy** provides a list of suggested extension activities.

The MiniReads

For struggling readers, trying to apply a new reading strategy to a challenging text can be frustrating and overwhelming. The reproducible MiniReads included in this resource offer a solution to this problem by providing short, easy-to-read, high-interest selections that students can use to "try out" new reading strategies. The MiniReads present a wide array of interdisciplinary topics.

The MiniReads contain **Active-Reading Questions** that draw students' attention to the Reading Skill and Reading Focus for the lesson, as well as other key features of the MiniRead. The questions allow students to pause and reflect as they read, use their prior knowledge, and check their comprehension. Space has been provided on each MiniRead page for students to write answers or take notes.

The Alternative Strategy Practice Worksheets

A worksheet is provided for the *Applying the Strategy* part of the lesson. The worksheets offer a variety of graphic organizers, focus questions or prompts, and group activities that help students practice the strategy with the MiniRead selection.

When Students Struggle with Reading, The Teacher Appears

Richard T. Vacca
Kent State University

The popular expression *struggling reader* often refers to low-achieving students who have major difficulties with reading. They lack fluency, have trouble decoding polysyllabic words, and make little sense of what they read. During my years as a high school English teacher, the students in my general, low-achieving classes were genuine in their resistance to reading. I knew where I stood with them. Teachers who have worked with low-achieving students are no strangers to resistant learners. All too often the low-achievers are overage, underprepared, and weighted down with emotional baggage. These students score low on proficiency tests and are tracked in basic classes for most of their academic lives.

Struggling readers can often be found "under cover" in English classrooms. They have developed a complex set of coping strategies to avoid reading or being held accountable for reading. These coping behaviors run the gamut from avoiding eye contact with the teacher, to disrupting lessons, to forgetting to bring books or assignments to class, to seeking help from friends. Attempting invisibility in English classrooms—the place where they might logically expect help—only serves to perpetuate a cycle of failure and ensures that they will remain helpless in many learning situations.

Put Yourself in Their Shoes

The real value of reading as a language activity lies in its uses. Whether we use reading to enter into the imaginative world of fiction; learn from academic texts; meet workplace demands; acquire insight and knowledge about people, places, and things; or understand a graphic on an Internet website, readers, to be successful, must adapt their skills and strategies to meet the comprehension demands of a particular task at hand. Reading is not as much a struggle as it is a challenge for those readers who know what to do.

Several years ago I developed a text passage to demonstrate how easy it is for good readers, such as you and I, to experience what it means to struggle with reading. More often than not, we approach the passage as a challenge and use a repertoire of reading strategies to construct meaning from the text. The passage, in the form of a short parable, poses a particular problem for readers as it tells the story of a king with kind but misguided intentions. The story begins:

> Once in the land of Serenity, there ruled a king called Kay Oss. The king wanted to be liked by all of his people. Onx day thx bxnxvolxnt dxspot dxcidxd that no onx in thx country would be rxsponsiblx for anything. So hx dxcrxxd zn xnd to work in his kingdom.
>
> Zll of thx workxrs rxstxd from thxvr dzvly lzbors. "Blxss Kvng Kxy Oss," thxy xxclzimxd! Thx fzrmxrs dvdn't hzrvxst thx crops. Thx Kvng's zrmy dvsbzndxd. Zll of thx mxrchznts vn thx kvngdom wxnt on zn xxtxndxd vzcztion to the Fzr Ezst. Thx shop ownxrs hung svgns on thxvr doors thzt szvd, "Gonx Fvshvng Vndxfvnvtxly."
>
> Nqw thx lzw mzkxrs vn thx lznd of Sxrxnvty wxrx vxry wvsx. But zs wvsx zs thxy wxrx, thxy dvd nqt wznt to zct zgzvnst thx kvng's wvshxs. Xvxn thxy stqppxd wqrkvng! So thx kvng dxcvdxd thzt thx bxst fqrm qf gqvxrnmxnt wzs nqnx zt zll. Zs tvmx wxnt qn, thx lznd of Sxrxnvty bxgzn tq splvt zt thx sxzms znd vt lqqkxd lvkx thvs: Bcx dqufghj klzm nqxp qqt rqst vqxwxxz bqxc dqf ghzj kqlxmmnxp.

As you read the story, did the substitution of the consonants *x*, *z*, *q*, and *v* for the vowels *e, a, o,* and *i* cause you to struggle a bit as a reader? Probably so. The progressive substitution of the consonants for vowels undoubtedly slowed down your *reading fluency*—the ability to read in a smooth, conversational manner—and may even have affected your accuracy in recognizing some words. Just think about some of the students in your classroom who struggle with reading. They may experience difficulty because they read in a slow and halting manner, word by word, and have trouble recognizing words quickly and accurately. They spend so much time and attention on trying to "say the words" that comprehension suffers and, as a result, the reading process breaks down for them.

Did you find this the case with the King Kay Oss passage? Probably not. Even though the substitution of consonants for vowels slowed you down a bit, chances are you were still able to comprehend the passage and construct meaning from it. This is because skilled readers do not use a single strategy to make sense of text. They know how to search for and make use of different types of information to construct meaning. Skilled readers have at their command *multiple strategies* for reading.

For example, as you read about King Kay Oss, you probably made some use of information clues among the letter/sound associations in the passage. Part of your ability to read, "Onx day thx bxnxvolxnt dxspot dxcidxd. . . ." depended on your recognition of some of the consonant and vowel letter/sound associations that were not altered in the passage. However, these letter/sound associations provide no clues to meaning. In order to construct meaning, you had to make use of other types of information in the passage. Your prior knowledge, including knowledge of syntax and grammatical relationships, helped you to anticipate some of the words in the passage which "had to come next" in order to sound like

language. For instance, as you read, "Zs tvmx _____ _____," you probably predicted that "went" and "on" would follow.

Moreover, skilled readers use prior knowledge to anticipate the meaning of known words or construct meaning for unknown words. Take another look at the third paragraph in the passage. As you read, "As time went on, the land of Serenity began to split at the seams and it looked like this:" you may have made the inference that "it" referred to Serenity and "this" referred to the string of unknown words that followed. These words convey no letter/sound or grammatical clues. They represent total confusion and disorder! By analogy, then, you may have inferred that the land of Serenity looked like it was in a state of total confusion and disorder much like the string of unknown words. Some skilled readers may even have concluded that there is a word to describe what happened in Serenity a long time ago. The word, in memory of King Kay Oss, is *chaos.*

Even the best of readers will struggle with reading at some time, in some place, with some text. A good reader on occasion will get lost in the writer's line of reasoning, or become confused by the way the text is organized, or run into unknown words that are difficult to pronounce let alone define. Perhaps main ideas are too difficult to grasp or the reader simply lacks prior knowledge to make connections to the important ideas in the text. Regardless of the comprehension problem, often it is only temporary. The difference between good readers and poor readers is that when good readers struggle with text, they know what to do to get out of trouble. When a text becomes confusing or does not make sense, good readers recognize that they have a repertoire of reading strategies at their command—alternatives—which they can use to work themselves out of difficulty.

Struggling Readers—A Closer Look

When I think of struggling readers, I'm reminded of the time Piglet was entirely surrounded by water in A. A. Milne's *The Pooh Story Book* (E.P. Dutton, 1965). It had rained and rained and rained. Piglet, alone in his house, is feeling more than a little worried because he is small and surrounded by water. As his anxiety mounts, Piglet reasons that his friends, Christopher Robin, Pooh, Kanga, Rabbit, Owl, and Eeyore, could easily escape the rapidly rising water by using their natural abilities. Christopher Robin and Pooh could climb trees, Kanga could jump, Rabbit could burrow, Owl could fly, and Eeyore could make a loud noise until rescued. Piglet concludes that he can't do *anything*.

Struggling readers feel much the same way. They experience Piglet's sense of helplessness on a daily basis in and out of school. Surrounded by a sea of print, they have few, if any, reading strategies to help them cope with the kinds of comprehension problems that must be solved to understand what they are reading.

Piglet thinks about his friends. What would they do under similar circumstances? Piglet is thinking strategically. He recognizes that his animal friends may not be high on the intelligence chain, but if surrounded by rapidly rising water, they would have a clever plan to get themselves out of trouble.

And so it is with struggling readers. They don't necessarily need high IQ's to get out of difficulty during reading. But what they do have to learn is how to work smart as readers. To work smart, struggling readers need to develop some control over reading strategies so that they too "will know what to do" to cope with difficult reading situations.

As Piglet thinks about what his friends would do, Christopher Robin appears—not physically, at least not yet, but in Piglet's mind.

He remembers a story that Christopher had told him about a man on a desert island who had written something in a bottle and thrown it in the sea. Buoyed by the memory, Piglet now has an alternative to doing nothing to save himself. The note in the bottle that Piglet throws into the water eventually makes its way to Pooh, who is confused by its contents but is wise enough to share the message with Christopher Robin. And as you might anticipate, Christopher Robin comes to Piglet's rescue just in the nick of time.

When students struggle with reading, the teacher appears. Through our instructional support and guidance, we can build students' confidence and competence as readers by showing them how to think strategically about reading and how to use reading strategies. Through *explanation, modeling, practice,* and *application* (the cornerstones of explicit instruction), we can help struggling students to develop alternatives to feeling helpless during reading. When teachers appear, they make explicit what good readers do to cope with the kinds of comprehension problems they encounter in their personal lives and in school.

How students achieve as readers reflects such factors as motivation, self-concept, prior knowledge, and the ability to use language to learn. For some struggling students, reading is a painful reminder of a system of schooling that has failed them. They wage a continual battle with reading as an academic activity. The failure to learn to read effectively has contributed to these students' disenchantment with and alienation from school. Although struggling readers may have developed some reading skills and strategies, these are often inappropriate for the demands inherent in potentially difficult texts. As a result, their participation in reading-related activities, such as writing or discussion, is marginal. Getting through reading assignments to answer homework questions is often the only reason to read, if they read at all.

"Learned helplessness" is an expression often associated with the struggling reader. It refers to students' perceptions of themselves as being unable to overcome failure. Unsuccessful readers usually sabotage their efforts to read by believing that they can't succeed at tasks that require reading. They struggle because they command a limited repertoire of strategies and lack knowledge of and control over the procedural routines needed to engage in meaningful transactions with texts. Rarely do struggling readers consider what their role should be as readers. Rather than take an active role in constructing meaning, they often remain passive and disengaged.

Not only do struggling readers lack competence with reading skills and strategies, they also lack confidence in their ability to make meaning with texts. They believe that they can't learn from reading. As a result, they are often ambivalent about the act of reading and fail to value what reading can do for them. For one reason or another, struggling readers have alienated themselves from the world of print.

Because reading is situational and depends on the task at hand, low-achieving students may not be the only ones who struggle with reading. Average and above-average students, even those on a fast track to go to college, might also struggle with reading. These students in particular are likely to conceal some of their difficulties with reading. Although they may have developed reading fluency, the ability to read print smoothly and accurately, average and above-average students who struggle as readers usually do not know what to do with texts. They appear *skillful* in the mechanics of reading but are not *strategic* in their ability to handle the comprehension demands inherent in the texts that they are reading.

National surveys of reading performance, such as the National Assessment of Educa-

tional Progress (NAEP), suggest that the majority of today's adolescents are capable of reading for literal understanding but have difficulty with more complex tasks. They struggle with what I call the ability to think with text. The *NAEP 1998 Reading Report Card for the Nation and the States* (Washington, D.C.: United States Department of Education) concluded that a majority of adolescents can read at *basic levels* of performance but have difficulty with more *advanced levels* of reading. Middle and high school students, for the most part, develop the "basics" of reading but do not know what to do with texts beyond just saying the words and attending to bits and pieces of information that they encounter during reading.

Reading Strategies

Students who struggle with texts, regardless of their ability level, often get lost in a maze of words as they sit down with a text assignment or scroll through an electronic page on a computer screen. The text does not make sense to them in ways that permit them to think deeply about the ideas they encounter as they read. One way to think about reading is to see it as a dialogue that takes place between the writer and the reader. But the talk usually is not the kind of loose, expressive language that might be used by two friends. The language of informational texts often is more formal than everyday language because the ideas these texts communicate often are complex and demanding. Reading is a strategic act, which is another way of saying that successful readers use *cognitive and metacognitive strategies* to engage in the dialogue so that they can understand, respond to, and even question and challenge the writer's ideas.

If struggling readers are fortunate, a teacher appears. We show up at the times when they most need us. Our "appearance" manifests itself through highly visible forms of instructional support which educational researchers have called *scaffolding.* Scaffolding instruction is one of the best ways I know to help students develop and become competent in the use of strategies they need to be successful readers. Used in construction, scaffolds serve as supports, lifting up workers so that they can achieve something that otherwise would not have been possible. Used as a metaphor in teaching and learning, scaffolding suggests support to help students to do what is not yet possible. Instructional scaffolding simply means giving students a better chance to be successful with texts than they would have if left on their own.

The Reading Workshops in *Elements of Language* scaffold instruction in the skills and strategies needed to read different types of writing in and out of school. The text selections for the workshops are both engaging and challenging for students at each grade level. Yet struggling readers may require additional instructional scaffolding in the development and use of reading skills and strategies. And this is where *Alternative Readings* can play a pivotal role in their development as readers.

Alternative Readings: An Instructional Resource for Struggling Readers

Struggling readers must have opportunities to practice and apply reading skills and strategies. We designed *Alternative Readings* for just that purpose. As an instructional resource, it provides teachers with alternative text selections (MiniReads) and reading strategies (Alternative Strategies) particularly suited for struggling readers. The MiniReads are shorter, easier texts than the Reading Selections in the Pupil's Editions of *Elements of Language*, but they are coordinated with those selections to provide experience with the same types of texts. They provide additional strategy practice for struggling readers. The Alternative Strategy lessons allow you to share insights and knowledge that students might otherwise never encounter. The strategy lessons in *Alternative Readings* follow an explicit instructional model as illustrated in the following diagram.

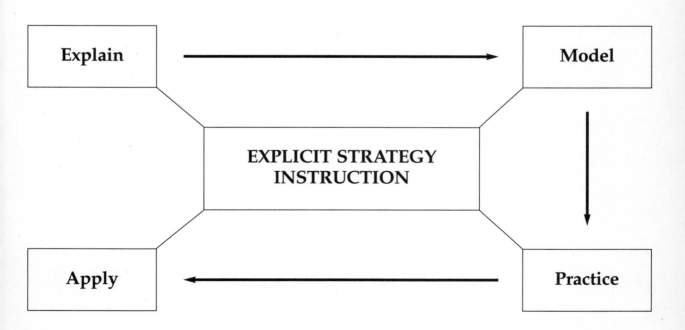

Explain	⟶	Model
EXPLICIT STRATEGY INSTRUCTION		
Apply	⟵	Practice

When Students Struggle with Reading, The Teacher Appears (continued)

Explicit instruction in the development and use of reading skills and strategies requires explanation, modeling, practice, and application.

- **EXPLAIN THE STRATEGY.** It is useful to struggling readers to be aware of the strategies. The lessons in *Alternative Readings* help to explain the rules, guidelines, or procedures associated with each strategy.

- **MODEL THE STRATEGY.** Explicit suggestions for modeling each strategy are provided in the teaching notes. These *think-alouds* allow the teacher to share with students the thinking processes involved in applying the strategy to a text.

- **PRACTICE THE STRATEGY.** The MiniReads provide students with easier texts, and the strategy explanations guide teachers to stop at key points in the MiniRead to ask questions and/or provide prompts. These questions and prompts mirror the thinking required to use the strategy effectively.

- **APPLY THE STRATEGY.** Once students have practiced an alternative strategy using a MiniRead selection, they are encouraged to apply the strategy in other reading situations, including the corresponding Reading Selection in *Elements of Language*.

When students struggle, the teacher appears. The explicit lessons in *Alternative Readings* create a framework that makes visible the instructional scaffolding that struggling readers need to develop control over reading strategies that can make a difference in their literate lives.

Reading an Eyewitness Account
Pupil's Edition, page 18

Overview

In order to identify the main idea of a text, students must analyze ideas and concepts and evaluate them in terms of their relative importance. Many students find this task bewildering; although they understand the details of the text, they have difficulty making the leap from simple comprehension of details to a synthesis of the main idea. Students may find descriptive pieces, such as eyewitness accounts, particularly difficult because main ideas are often implied rather than directly stated.

This lesson includes

- an eyewitness account **MiniRead,** including **Active-Reading Questions** (page 4)
- an **Alternative Strategy** for teaching eyewitness accounts to struggling readers (page 2)
- an **Alternative Strategy Practice** worksheet for students to apply the strategy and skill to the MiniRead (page 6)

MiniRead Summary: "Going . . . Going . . . Gone!"

This eyewitness account describes a fan's experience of watching baseball star Mark McGwire break a 37-year-old home-run record. Using descriptive language, the writer evokes the excitement of the crowd, the camaraderie of the players, and the specific action of the play. While the atmosphere of the exciting moment is an important idea in the MiniRead, the writer also implies that the good sportsmanship of Sammy Sosa, McGwire's friend and rival, was essential to the good feeling of the game.

Using the MiniRead

BEFORE READING Students can preview the MiniRead by looking at the title and scanning the text for descriptive words and phrases. What do the descriptions suggest? Have students experienced places or events that could be described similarly?

DURING READING Students may want to work in pairs to read and answer the questions or take turns reading portions of the MiniRead aloud before they answer each question. They can write their responses in the margins of the MiniRead.

AFTER READING Students can complete the **Alternative Strategy Practice** worksheet by completing the first section independently, then discussing their word choices in small groups before finishing the worksheet.

USING THE MINIREAD WITH THE PUPIL'S EDITION

After students have read and discussed the MiniRead, they may be better prepared to read the Reading Selection, "Hopi Snake Ceremonies," in the Pupil's Edition. If the MiniRead is taught in place of the Reading Selection, students will still be able to complete the Mini-Lessons and Writing Workshop.

Reading an Eyewitness Account *(continued)*

Most Important Word

To use the Most Important Word strategy, students read a text and decide which word they think is the most significant. Then they use the word in a sentence that expresses the main idea of the text. Students support their choices using evidence from the text. After students have chosen their words and written their main idea statements, they discuss in small groups their words and explanations.

Modeling the Strategy

After students have read the MiniRead, choose a passage from it that is rich in description and read the passage aloud. For instance, you might choose paragraph 4:

> The action peaked in the fourth inning of the game when the Cardinals were batting. McGwire sprang to the plate for his second time at bat. Fifty thousand fans seemed to jump to their feet all at once. The earsplitting cheers began. Around the stadium I saw thousands of red Cardinal jerseys and joyful smiles. Cameras began flashing. For a minute the field looked more like a laser-light show than a baseball game.

Choose an important word from the paragraph, and explain your reasons for choosing it, citing evidence from the text. Then, formulate a main idea statement using the word. Students can comment on your choice and reasons. You might say, "I think the most important word is *peaked*. The paragraph says that the fans jumped to their feet and began cheering and that they were smiling. This seems like the peak of the action of the game. I think the main idea is that the excitement of the game reached a peak when Mark McGwire stepped up for his second turn at the plate."

Applying the Strategy

Students should understand that there is no one "right" most important word. Their objective is to support their choices with evidence from the MiniRead and then to formulate a main idea statement for the MiniRead, using the word. Students should complete the worksheet, then discuss in small groups their words, explanations, and main idea statements. Some students may change their words or main idea statements after arriving at a clearer understanding of the text through group discussion.

STRATEGY OPTIONS

Students may want to choose a word for different sections of the MiniRead, then narrow their choices to a single word. They can use the margin of the MiniRead to note possible most important words as they read.

Students can try to agree on one main idea statement for the group, and then each group can discuss its statement with the class.

To facilitate discussion of most important words, group students who have chosen different words. Alternatively, you can group students who have chosen the same word and have them discuss how to persuade other groups to accept their choice.

Reading an Eyewitness Account *(continued)*

Extending the Strategy

You may want to have students

- discuss how the strategy helped them identify the main idea of the MiniRead
- apply the strategy to the Reading Selection in the Pupil's Edition
- apply the strategy to other types of texts, such as newspaper articles or other descriptive writing

Mini Read

Going … Going … Gone!

DIRECTIONS Write your answers to the questions in the space below.

I love going to major league baseball games. I love the spicy smell of ballpark hot dogs and the flashing colors on the giant message boards. The booming music on the loudspeakers invites me to sing and clap along. I can feel electricity in the air as thousands of fans cheer for their favorite players.

1. How does the writer help you experience the sights, sounds, and smells of the ballpark?

One baseball game I went to will always stand out. It was played at Busch Stadium in St. Louis, Missouri, on September 8, 1998. The St. Louis Cardinals were playing against the Chicago Cubs. That night Mark McGwire of the Cardinals had a chance to hit his sixty-second home run of the season and break a home-run record that had stood for thirty-seven years.

2. Based on this paragraph, what do you think this essay might be about?

McGwire's friend and rival for the record, Sammy Sosa, was playing for the Chicago Cubs. Sammy needed four more home runs to break the record himself.

All summer long I had watched these two awesome rivals race for the home-run record. I admired them as they shook hands, joked with sportscasters, and grinned with delight at their accomplishments. Game after game their home-run totals inched closer and closer to the magic number 62. In a way, "Mighty Mac" and "Slammin' Sammy" had become like brothers who shared a goal, but only one of them could win. Which man would become the new home-run king? This burning question was on everyone's mind at Busch Stadium on September 8.

3. What is the mood being conveyed in this paragraph?

The action peaked in the fourth inning of the game when the Cardinals were batting. McGwire sprang to the plate for his second time at bat. Fifty thousand fans seemed to jump to their feet all at once. The earsplitting cheers began. Around the stadium I saw thousands of red Cardinal jerseys and joyful smiles. Cameras began flashing. For a minute the field looked more like a laser-light show than a baseball game.

4. Here and in the next paragraph, what details describe the scene at the ballpark? What quality or feeling do the details create?

The Cub's pitcher, Steve Trachsel, pitched a sinking fastball. The ball traveled at 88 miles per hour. With huge arms like Popeye's,

Going ... Going ... Gone! *(continued)*

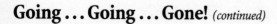

McGwire swung the bat and smashed the ball to left field. The hit was a low line drive that looked as if it might not make it out of the ballpark. At that moment everyone in the stadium seemed to lean forward together to watch the ball. Was this the magic sixty-second, or would the ball fall short of the left-field wall? For a few heart-stopping seconds, we all watched in suspense.

Suddenly, we knew. McGwire shot both arms over his head and pumped his fist. The ball had cleared the wall, just barely. McGwire hugged the first-base coach. In his excitement, he leaped over first base, almost forgetting to touch the bag. He ran the rest of the bases and gave high-fives to the Cub infielders. I looked out in right

> **5.** Why do you think the writer included the details about Sosa's reaction?

field and saw Sammy Sosa clapping his hand into his glove. Then he touched his heart and gave McGwire a happy two-finger salute.

McGwire jumped onto home plate. He pointed up to the crowd and then turned to greet his teammates. The Cardinals were streaming out of the dugout to mob him. In the sky, fireworks exploded over the stadium. A message board flashed "An American dream comes true." The celebration had begun.

Although McGwire won the home-run race, Sammy Sosa was also a hero that night. After McGwire rounded the bases, Sosa streaked in from right field and grabbed McGwire in a joyful bearhug. Then Sosa flashed his fellow slugger a grin that seemed to shout "Well done, my friend!"

Up in the stands, the crowd was still going wild. Excitement rang through the stadium. We were laughing and crying at the same time.

> **6.** According to the writer, why was this baseball game important?

Cubs fans and Cardinals fans were hugging each other like long-lost friends. "I can't believe I'm really here," I thought. "I just saw two of the world's greatest sports heroes make baseball history." The best part was that both McGwire and Sosa seemed like winners.

Most Important Word

DIRECTIONS Use these steps to apply the **Most Important Word** strategy to the MiniRead, "Going . . . Going . . . Gone!"

▶ **STEP 1: Choose a word.**

- The most important word in the MiniRead is _____.

▶ **STEP 2: Explain your choice.**

- Write several reasons why you chose this word.
  Use examples from the MiniRead to support your choice.

▶ **STEP 3: Write.**

- Based on the word you chose, write a sentence that states the main idea of the MiniRead:

▶ **STEP 4: Discuss.**

- In a small group, discuss each member's (1) word choice, (2) reasons for the choice, and (3) main idea statement.

- After the discussion, did you change your mind about the most important word and main idea?

  _____ yes   _____ no

  Explain why or why not in the space below.

Reading Instructions

Pupil's Edition, page 50

Reading Skill

Identifying Author's Purpose

Reading Focus

Order of a Process

Overview

To understand instructions, students need to know how to identify an author's purpose and follow the order of the process being described. Some students may understand the individual steps but get bogged down when they try to reexplain the steps or remember them in order. Since instructions written in essay form often have a dual purpose—not just to convey facts but also to entertain or influence the reader—students need to both understand and evaluate this mode.

This lesson includes

- an instructions **MiniRead,** including **Active-Reading Questions** (page 9)
- an **Alternative Strategy** for teaching instructions to struggling readers (page 8)
- an **Alternative Strategy Practice** worksheet for students to apply the strategy and skill to the MiniRead (page 12)

MiniRead Summary: "The Crabmaster"

These instructions for eating a crab are both informative and entertaining. The writer describes some animals' methods of eating crabs, then explains how humans should approach the task: with lots of newspapers for the mess and some tools for cracking the shells and extracting the meat.

Using the MiniRead

NOTE: The Alternative Strategy on the next page guides students through a prereading activity.

BEFORE READING Students can preview the MiniRead by looking at the title and illustrations and scanning the text and questions. What do they already know about crabs? Have they eaten other crustaceans, such as lobster? What could a "crabmaster" be? Ask students to predict the author's purpose for writing the MiniRead.

DURING READING Students may want to work in pairs to read and answer the questions or take turns reading portions of the MiniRead aloud before they answer each question. They can write their responses in the margins of the MiniRead.

AFTER READING Students can respond to the statements on the **Alternative Strategy Practice** worksheet in groups or as a class, before and after reading the MiniRead. Then they can discuss as a class or in small groups whether their predictions about the author's purpose were correct.

USING THE MINIREAD WITH THE PUPIL'S EDITION

After students have read and discussed the MiniRead, they may be better prepared to read the Reading Selection, "The Voice in the Attic," in the Pupil's Edition. If the MiniRead is taught in place of the Reading Selection in the Pupil's Edition, students will still be able to complete the Mini-Lessons and Writing Workshop.

Reading Instructions *(continued)*

Anticipation Guides

Before reading a text, students read statements related to the subject of the text and to the author's purpose. They decide whether they agree or disagree with each statement. After reading the selection, students respond to the statements again to see if their opinions changed after reading.

Modeling the Strategy

Before students read the MiniRead, make a generalization such as, "It's not worth the trouble to eat messy foods." Ask students whether they agree or disagree with the statement. Some students may disagree strongly and name specific messy-to-eat foods that they like. Others may agree and say that they don't like to get taco sauce all over their hands when they eat tacos or fruit juice on their hands when they eat oranges. Still others may find some foods worth the trouble and others not. Then, have students read the first two paragraphs of "The Crabmaster." Ask whether any of them have changed their minds about the generalization.

Applying the Strategy

Students should complete Step 1 of the worksheet before reading the MiniRead. After reading, students should complete Step 2 by responding to the statements again to see if their opinions changed. Then, in small groups, students can share their responses, using specific examples from the MiniRead to support their opinions. Students should be aware that there are no "right" answers to the statements.

Extending the Strategy

You may want to have students

- discuss how the strategy helped them identify the author's purpose
- summarize the steps in the instructions given by the author
- apply the strategy to the Reading Selection in the Pupil's Edition
- apply the strategy to other types of texts, using Anticipation Guides you provide

The Crabmaster

DIRECTIONS Write your answers to the questions in the space below.

Eating a steamed crab is not exactly a day at the beach. How can anything that tastes so good be so hard to eat? Wild animals have figured out ways to get inside the crab's spiky shell. Some animals wait for the time every year when the crab sheds its old hard shell and grows a new soft one. Other animals, like sea otters, simply smash the crab against a rock and gobble down the meat.

Humans have a much harder time eating crabs, but the sweet-tasting meat is our reward. Crabs are also a great source of nutrition. A crab is high in protein and has only about eighty-five calories. Mastering the art of crab eating is messy but fun. Learn the trick, and you can enjoy sharing a crab dinner with family and friends.

1. What might be the author's reason for writing about this topic?

Do not eat crabs in a fancy restaurant or dining room. Instead, set up a picnic table and cover it with newspaper. While you're at it, cover the floor, too. You will need a bunch of napkins or paper towels. Most important, you will need tools for attacking the crab's shell and getting out the meat. A nutcracker or mallet, like a hammer, works well to crack the shell. A small knife helps slice through the claws. Then, to poke the meat out of the shell, you will need a small fork or pick. If you are eating crabs steamed in spices, you will want lots of water to cool your mouth. You may also want a bowl of water nearby to give your spice-covered crab a dunking.

2. What can you conclude about eating crabs from reading this paragraph?

First, dive into the bag or pot full of steamed crabs and pull one out. Be ready for what you will see. A crab is not a pretty sight. It

The Crabmaster *(continued)*

has spidery legs, pointy claws, a jagged shell, and beady eyes. Begin with the easy parts: the legs. They do not have much meat in them, but they are fun to eat. Snap the legs off the body. Then you can split them open easily with your fingers. Next, use a thin fork to poke out the meat inside the legs. You can also pretend the leg is a straw and suck the meat out. At this point, begin a garbage pile of shells.

3. Could the step described in this paragraph come after the step in the next paragraph? Why or why not?

After the legs, you have a choice. You can go for the easy-to-eat claws or tackle the hardest part, the body. To do claws, twist one off the body. The claw has pincers at the end, like pliers. Split open the claw using a nutcracker, or use a mallet and small knife. Hold the knife with the

4. In your own words, describe how to eat a crab claw.

blade pointing down just behind the joint where the pincers join, and then bang the mallet on the knife's other end. The knife blade should slice through the shell. If you are lucky, the claw will split open, and the meat will be right there for the eating. If not, you can just smash the shell—kind of like an otter would—and pick the shell fragments off the meat. Then, eat the second claw using the same method.

Mallet for pounding

Last comes the biggest challenge: the body. Some crab eaters do not bother with the body, but you cannot be a true Crabmaster without it. First, turn the body over and look for a small piece in the middle of the crab's belly. This piece, called the "apron," looks a little like the tab on a pop-top aluminum can. Gently push the apron up. Next, carefully pry the top and bottom shells apart to get inside the crab. Here you will need to stop and take a deep breath. The inside

The Crabmaster *(continued)*

of a crab looks pretty disgusting. You will see mushy intestines. You will also see the spongy, grayish gills that crabs breathe through. Do not eat these parts. Just say "yuck" and scoop them out onto your shell pile. Then, wipe your fingers and enjoy your meal. Most of what is left is delicious white crab meat to pick out piece by piece.

5. What details and examples does the author include here to explain how to eat the body?

At the end, you will be sitting in front of a slimy newspaper with a pile of garbage to one side. You will have shell bits in your hair and a burning mouth if your crabs were spicy. Take a big gulp of water, reach for another crab, and congratulate yourself. You have gained a great talent. You are the Crabmaster.

Anticipation Guides

DIRECTIONS Use these steps to help you identify the author's purpose in the MiniRead, "The Crabmaster."

STEP 1:
Before reading "The Crabmaster," read the statements below and decide whether you agree or disagree with each statement. Circle the appropriate word in each "Before Reading" section. Be ready to explain your opinion.

1. Reading a set of instructions is boring.	**Before Reading:** AGREE DISAGREE	**After Reading:** AGREE DISAGREE
2. Step-by-step instructions should give the steps in the exact order in which they should be done.	**Before Reading:** AGREE DISAGREE	**After Reading:** AGREE DISAGREE
3. Factual articles are written to convey information, not for fun.	**Before Reading:** AGREE DISAGREE	**After Reading:** AGREE DISAGREE
4. A good set of instructions does not include any unnecessary information.	**Before Reading:** AGREE DISAGREE	**After Reading:** AGREE DISAGREE

STEP 2:
After reading "The Crabmaster," read the statements again and circle the appropriate word in each "After Reading" section.

STEP 3:
Respond to the following questions in the space provided.

1. What was the author's purpose for writing this text (to inform, to persuade, to entertain, and/or to describe)?

2. What details from the MiniRead help the reader to determine the author's purpose?

Reading an Advantages/Disadvantages Article
Pupil's Edition, page 82

Reading Skill

Making Inferences: Drawing Conclusions

Reading Focus

Advantage/Disadvantages Structure

Overview

Many students have difficulty weighing the pros and cons expressed in a text to reach a conclusion. This task is especially difficult when the writer does not state a definite opinion, which is often the case in an advantages/disadvantages article. These readers often need practice analyzing and evaluating details in a text in order to draw conclusions about the information presented.

This lesson includes

- an advantages/disadvantages **MiniRead,** including **Active-Reading Questions** (page 16)
- an **Alternative Strategy** for teaching advantages/disadvantages articles to struggling readers (page 14)
- an **Alternative Strategy Practice** worksheet for students to apply the strategy and skill to the MiniRead (page 19)

MiniRead Summary: "To e, or Not to e"

The writer discusses the pros and cons of using e-mail rather than other means of communication, such as letters and telephone calls. Among the advantages of e-mail are speed, multiple-copy capability, convenience, and ease of revision. Disadvantages include computer-related e-mail breakdowns, garbled messages, the number of people who don't have e-mail addresses, and the impersonal format. The writer concludes that although e-mail is useful, it is not always superior to older forms of communication.

Using the MiniRead

BEFORE READING Students can preview the MiniRead by looking at the title, illustrations, and section heads. What is the topic of the MiniRead? What do the section heads imply about the writer's opinions of this topic?

DURING READING Students may want to work in pairs to read and answer the questions or take turns reading portions of the MiniRead aloud before they answer each question. They can write their responses in the margins of the MiniRead.

AFTER READING Students can complete the **Alternative Strategy Practice** worksheet on their own before discussing their sketches in small groups.

USING THE MINIREAD WITH THE PUPIL'S EDITION

After students have read and discussed the MiniRead, they may be better prepared to read the Reading Selection, "For Girls Only?" in the Pupil's Edition. If the MiniRead is taught in place of the Reading Selection, students will still be able to complete the Mini-Lessons and Writing Workshop.

Reading an Advantages/Disadvantages Article (continued)

Sketch to Stretch

To use this strategy, students read a text and then create drawings to represent a conclusion they have drawn from the text. Students write explanations of their sketches, using specific evidence from the text to support their conclusions. Each student presents his or her drawing to a small group, and the group discusses the meaning of the drawing and its relation to the text. Then the student explains the sketch and his or her conclusion to the group.

Modeling the Strategy

Students should understand that the sketch is not an illustration or a literal representation of the text, but rather a symbolic drawing that represents a conclusion that can be drawn about information in the text. If you have used this strategy previously, show students a sample sketch that a student drew after reading a text. If this strategy is new to your students, you may need to show a sample sketch based on a text with which students are familiar. You might use the following passage as an example.

> Archaeologists are people who study ancient human cultures by looking closely at historical remains and artifacts, such as tools, jewelry, and pottery. Many artifacts and architectural features do not survive. Those made of wood, cloth, and leather often rot. Stone buildings tumble, and the stones are used for other purposes. In addition, some ancient cultures pass on their knowledge by word of mouth, leaving behind very few records of their way of life.

You might draw a simple sketch of a stick figure wearing an adventure-style hat and placing a puzzle piece in a rectangular puzzle that is still missing several pieces.

Explanation: I drew an archaeologist putting together puzzle pieces because that's what archaeology is like: figuring out an ancient culture with the help of clues, such as artifacts. Some of the pieces are still missing, though, because there are still some things the archaeologist does not know.

Conclusion: Archaeologists face difficulties trying to figure out what an ancient culture was like, because artifacts only tell part of the story.

Reading an Advantages/Disadvantages Article *(continued)*

STRATEGY OPTIONS

Alternatively, students can discuss the MiniRead with a partner and collaborate on a sketch.

Students who have trouble starting their sketches may want to do a few practice drawings on scrap paper before they put their sketches on the worksheet.

After sharing their sketches in small groups, students may have a class discussion in which representatives from each group share the conclusions drawn by group members.

Applying the Strategy

Students should complete the worksheet, then take turns sharing and responding in small groups. Students should be sure to withhold their explanations of their own drawings until the rest of the group has had a chance to respond to the drawing. Then the student can tell the group his or her reasons for what appears in the sketch.

Extending the Strategy

You may want to have students

- discuss how the strategy helped them understand the advantages and disadvantages discussed in the MiniRead
- discuss how the strategy helped them make inferences
- apply the strategy to the Reading Selection in the Pupil's Edition
- apply the strategy to other types of texts, such as short stories, poems, and opinion pieces

To *e*, or Not to *e*

When the Internet was created, it gave people a brand-new question to ask: "Hey, what's your e-mail address?" A new form of communication had been born, called electronic mail, or "e-mail" for short. Millions of people began sending e-mailed letters and messages through their computers instead of writing letters and making telephone calls. E-mail created an explosion of new addresses full of strange *www*'s, *dot com*'s, and @'s. This way of communicating caught on quickly because it combined many advantages of letters and telephones without some of the disadvantages. Does e-mail's popularity prove it is the best form of communication? Judge for yourself.

> **1.** What topic is the writer going to be discussing in this article?

Wildly Popular . . .

E-mail shares some advantages with letters. It allows you to organize and express your thoughts in writing. You can figure out what you want to say without anyone watching or listening, so you will not feel rushed. Then you can look back over what you have written and decide to make changes before anyone reads it. Another benefit is that your reader can re-read the message you sent as often as he or she wants. The message can be read on the computer screen or printed out.

> **2.** In the first three paragraphs of this section, the writer compares e-mail and letters. What are the good points that e-mail shares with letters? In what ways is sending e-mail better than writing letters?

E-mail has some big advantages over handwritten letters sent by regular mail. With letters you have to write neatly so others can read your handwriting. If you need to cross out a mistake, you often start the letter over. With e-mail, because you write on a computer, you can easily make changes and correct mistakes without starting over.

Another great feature of e-mail is that you can easily send copies to more than one person. Plus, if you

To *e*, or Not to *e* *(continued)*

want your reader to refer to earlier e-mails, you can include them as part of your new e-mail. In fact, your e-mail can drag a whole train of earlier letters behind it. You can also attach other electronic documents to your e-mail without paying for copies or postage.

One big advantage e-mail shares with the telephone is speed. E-mail is almost as quick as a phone call and much quicker than a "snail-mail" letter. You do not have to wait days, weeks, or months for a reply. Often you will hear back right away or within a few hours. In some ways, e-mail is better than a phone call. Your reader can choose when to open and read your e-mail. You do not risk calling and bothering someone who does not want to talk right then.

> **3.** Based on this paragraph, is e-mail better than a phone call? Explain your answer.

. . . But Has Drawbacks

The bad side of e-mail is that sometimes it simply does not work. Weather, satellite problems, and strange computer errors can cause an e-mail breakdown. "Your mailbox cannot be accessed at this time." Most e-mail users have seen these or similar words come up on the computer screen.

> **4.** Does this section discuss advantages or disadvantages? How do you know?

You cannot assume everyone has an e-mail address, since not everyone is hooked up to the Internet. Another downside is that you cannot assume that what you send through e-mail will be exactly what your reader receives. The format of e-mails can change as they zip over the Internet. The complex chart you worked on so hard can arrive as an unreadable mess.

Some people would say the biggest drawback to e-mail is that it seems cold and unfriendly. With e-mail we lose the personal connection of hearing someone's voice, talking directly to another human being, or holding in our hand a letter with real writing from someone else's hand.

Is There a "Best"?

Is e-mail the best form of communication? Often people have their own reasons for choosing one form over another. E-mail clearly has advantages and disadvantages. It has given us a speedy way to move information across great distances. On the other hand, it is not

always dependable, and it may have a negative effect on human relationships. So don't throw away your stamps and envelopes yet, and remember to keep paying your phone bill.

5. After reading the concluding paragraph, what ideas do you have about e-mail as a type of communication?

Sketch to Stretch

DIRECTIONS Use these steps to help you draw conclusions about the MiniRead,
"To *e*, or Not to *e*."

> **STEP 1:**
> After reading the MiniRead, draw in the space below a sketch that represents a con-
> clusion you made based on the MiniRead. You may want to do a few practice draw-
> ings before you put your final sketch on the worksheet.

▶ **STEP 2:**

In the space below, write an explanation of your sketch. Then, write your conclusions, using specific evidence from the MiniRead to support your conclusions.

My Explanation:

My Conclusions:

Reading a Novel's Book Jacket

Pupil's Edition, page 118

Reading Skill

Questioning and Predicting

Reading Focus

Preview Information

Overview

Previewing a novel by examining its jacket allows the reader to predict the novel's subject matter, assess its interest level, and read more actively by formulating questions to answer while reading. Students often have trouble previewing a novel because they haven't figured out how to analyze and evaluate the information on a book jacket to make predictions.

This lesson includes

- a book-jacket **MiniRead,** including **Active-Reading Questions** (page 24)
- an **Alternative Strategy** for teaching book jackets to struggling readers (page 22)
- an **Alternative Strategy Practice** worksheet for students to apply the strategy and skill to the MiniRead (page 28).

MiniRead Summary: Book Jacket

The MiniRead consists of a sample book jacket for the novel *Julie of the Wolves* by Jean Craighead George, including back-cover blurbs, a plot summary (not revealing the ending) on the front flap, and brief biographies of the author and illustrator on the back flap. The novel is about a thirteen-year-old Alaskan Eskimo girl who undertakes a harrowing journey to escape the traditional arranged marriage that her elders want for her. She gets lost, is rescued by a pack of wolves, and must choose between life with the wolves and life among people.

Using the MiniRead

NOTE: The Alternative Strategy on the next page guides students through a during-reading activity.

BEFORE READING Students can preview the MiniRead by looking at the title and illustrations, scanning the text, and formulating questions about the topic. What does the title reveal about the plot? What does the heading "Winner of the 1973 Newbery Medal" tell us about the book?

DURING READING Students may want to work in pairs to read and answer the questions or take turns reading portions of the MiniRead aloud before they answer each question. They can write their responses in the margins of the MiniRead.

AFTER READING Students can complete the **Alternative Strategy Practice** worksheet in pairs before they discuss their responses with the rest of the class.

USING THE MINIREAD WITH THE PUPIL'S EDITION

After students have read and discussed the MiniRead, they may be better prepared to read the Reading Selection, a book jacket for *Crash,* in the Pupil's Edition. If the MiniRead is taught in place of the Reading Selection, students will still be able to complete the Mini-Lessons and Writing Workshop.

Reading a Novel's Book Jacket *(continued)*

Say Something

To use this strategy, students work with partners. As they read silently or aloud, they stop at designated points in the text and take turns beginning a discussion by "saying something" about what they have just read. In their conversations, students can make a prediction, make a comment, ask a question, or make a connection. Students might mention something they didn't understand or were curious about. (If students can't think of anything to say, they should re-read the passage.)

Modeling the Strategy

Write the following four words on the board: *predict, comment, question, connect.* Read aloud a passage from the MiniRead that gives clues about the novel; then, make sample Say Something comments. The following is an excerpt from the book jacket's back cover with sample comments that you might make.

> The author is a naturalist who has observed wolves at first hand. Her novel is packed with expert wolf lore, its narrative beautifully conveying the sweeping vastness of tundra as well as many other aspects of the Arctic, ancient and modern, animal and human.
> —*The New York Times*

Prediction: "I think this novel takes place in the Arctic and has something to do with wolves."

Question: "How can wolves be characters in a novel?"

Comment: "I think *The New York Times* has good book reviews, so I am inclined to believe what this reviewer says."

Connection: "This reminds me of another book I read by an author who was an expert on wolves; his book was full of interesting information."

As you make each type of remark about the sample passage, put a check mark next to the corresponding label on the board. Students should feel free to respond to your remarks. Then, encourage students to make other Say Something comments about the passage. As students comment, place a check mark under the correct category on the board to indicate the type of comment.

Reading a Novel's Book Jacket *(continued)*

STRATEGY OPTIONS

You may need to point out to students that questions they ask can be about anything they don't understand in the text. For instance, they might ask something as simple as, "What does this word mean?"

Encourage students to be specific in their conversations and to refer to the text to try to answer questions they might have. Students might find this easier if, as they read each section, they underline portions of the text that they want to talk about or don't understand.

After completing the worksheet, students can discuss as a class their predictions about what the book is about and whether it sounds interesting, as well as any unanswered questions they might have.

Applying the Strategy

Students should complete Step 1 of the worksheet with a partner as they read the MiniRead. When students begin a conversation about a section of the text, they can first answer the active-reading question(s) that pertain to that section, then ask any questions they might have and make comments, predictions, or connections. Encourage students to make various types of comments in their conversations. Students can complete Step 2 of the worksheet individually or with their partners.

Extending the Strategy

You may want to have students

- discuss how the strategy helped them make predictions about the novel
- discuss the helpfulness of stopping several times in the text to talk with a partner
- apply the strategy to the Reading Selection in the Pupil's Edition
- apply the strategy to book jackets from other novels

DIRECTIONS Write your answers to the questions in the space below.

1. What do the title and illustration suggest about the book?

JULIE OF THE WOLVES

Jean Craighead George

Winner
of the 1973
Newbery
Medal

Cover illustration by Robert Parton

FRONT COVER

JULIE OF THE WOLVES

Winner of the 1973 Newbery Medal

"A compelling story about thirteen-year-old Julie Edwards Miyax Kapugen, an Eskimo girl caught between the old ways and those of the whites, between childhood and womanhood. Jean George has captured the subtle nuances of Eskimo life, animal habits, the pain of growing up, and combines these elements into a thrilling adventure which is, at the same time, a poignant love story."
—*School Library Journal*

"The author is a naturalist who has observed wolves at first hand. Her novel is packed with expert wolf lore, its narrative beautifully conveying the sweeping vastness of tundra as well as many other aspects of the Arctic, ancient and modern, animal and human."
—*The New York Times*

Trade ISBN 0-06-021943-2
Library ISBN 0-06-021944-0

> **2.** What do the phrases "thrilling adventure" and "poignant love story" suggest about the events in the book?

BACK COVER

Most people call her Miyax. Her pen pal in San Francisco calls her Julie. Julie is a thirteen-year-old Eskimo girl living in a small Eskimo village in Alaska. Her mother is dead, and her father is missing. Elders from her village force her into an arranged marriage, but she runs away from its misery. She plans to head south toward faraway California to find her pen pal, Amy. When winter sets in, Julie becomes lost in the wilderness of the Alaskan North Slope. She is completely alone and feels weak from hunger. Then she meets a pack of wolves. Watching them closely, Julie learns how to make them accept her into the pack. To survive in the wilderness she takes on a new identity. She learns to think like a wolf and grows to love her new companions. Finally, Julie must choose between the wolves she loves and the modern world.

This inspiring coming-of-age story describes the experiences of a young girl caught between two worlds. It is an exciting tale of strength, survival, friendship, and oneness with nature that no reader will ever forget.

> **3.** What problems does Julie face in the book? Would you be interested in finding out how she solves them?

FRONT FLAP

Jean Craighead George has written dozens of books in which she shares her lifelong love of nature with young readers. Born in 1919 in Washington, D.C., she spent her summers at her family's Pennsylvania farm. There she learned about creatures ranging from possums to owls and falcons. After she graduated from Pennsylvania State University, Jean Craighead married John George. Jean and her husband wrote several children's books about animals. Then, Jean began to write on her own. Her first novel, *My Side of the Mountain,* was a huge success. She wrote *Julie of the Wolves* (1972) after a trip to Alaska, where she studied the behavior of a wolf pack. The character of Julie was inspired by a small Eskimo child Jean saw who was walking into the wilderness by herself. The book won the distinguished Newbery Medal in 1973 and has since become a classic.

Robert Parton was born in Philadelphia, Pennsylvania. As a boy, he loved copying detailed drawings of wolves, foxes, and dogs from old library books. He decided to become an artist and studied at the Pennsylvania Academy of the Fine Arts. True to his early interest, Parton has specialized in drawing wolves and dogs.

BACK FLAP

4. Do you think the author of this book has enough knowledge to write about wolves? Why or why not?

5. How did Jean George get the idea for this book?

6. What interests do Jean George and Robert Parton have in common?

Say Something

DIRECTIONS Use these steps to apply the **Say Something** strategy to the MiniRead.

STEP 1:
Read the book jacket for *Julie of the Wolves* with a partner, pausing at the end of each section (front cover, back cover, front flap, and back flap) to "say something" about what you have just read. Put a check mark in the appropriate category of the chart below as you make each type of comment.

Predict	Comment	Question	Connect

STEP 2:
After you finish your conversations, answer the questions below in the space provided.

1. Which of the four types of comments above did you and your partner make most often? Why do you think this happened?

2. What questions about the text were you and your partner able to answer by having a discussion?

3. Based on your conversations, what do you predict about the events that take place in *Julie of the Wolves?*

Reading an Informative Article
Pupil's Edition, page 158

Reading Skill

Summarizing Information

Reading Focus

Textbook Features

Overview

To summarize an informative article, students must be able to distinguish between central ideas and supporting details. They also need to understand the central ideas well enough to be able to describe them in their own words. Some students have difficulty creating summaries of articles, not only because they struggle with comprehension but also because they have trouble seeing how each fact functions within the text.

This lesson includes

- an informative article **MiniRead,** including **Active-Reading Questions** (page 32)
- an **Alternative Strategy** for teaching informative articles to struggling readers (page 30)
- an **Alternative Strategy Practice** worksheet for students to apply the strategy and skill to the MiniRead (page 34)

MiniRead Summary: "News from *Galileo*"

The article describes the three major discoveries made by the spacecraft *Galileo*, which reached Jupiter in 1995. The first discovery is that Europa, one of the moons of Jupiter, contains liquid water. The second discovery is that there is heat, possibly created by the motion of tides, on Europa. The third discovery is that Europa may contain organic compounds. Liquid water, heat, and organic compounds are the conditions under which life can develop. As far as we know, they have come together in only one other place—Earth.

Using the MiniRead

BEFORE READING Students can preview the MiniRead by looking at the title, headings, underlined words, and footnotes and thinking about their prior knowledge of the topic. What do they already know about the solar system?

DURING READING Students may want to work in pairs to read and answer the questions or take turns reading portions of the MiniRead aloud before they answer each question. They can write their responses in the margins of the MiniRead.

AFTER READING Students can complete the **Alternative Strategy Practice** worksheet in small groups before exchanging summaries as a class.

USING THE MINIREAD WITH THE PUPIL'S EDITION

After students have read and discussed the MiniRead, they may be better prepared to read the Reading Selection, "The Body's Defenses," in the Pupil's Edition. If the MiniRead is taught in place of the Reading Selection, students will still be able to complete the Mini-Lessons and Writing Workshop.

Reading an Informative Article *(continued)*

Magnet Summaries

To use this strategy, students read a text and write down a few (usually three to four) "magnet words," or words they consider central to the text's meaning. Students write each of these words on a 3" x 5" card, then surround each word with the supporting details that relate to it. Then students use each card to form a sentence that summarizes a section of the text, using the magnet word and supporting details. Students strive to condense the words and phrases on each card, but they may use two sentences if necessary. Finally, students combine their individual sentences, making the necessary adjustments in wording, to construct an overall summary of the text.

Modeling the Strategy

After students have read the MiniRead, choose a passage from it that contains a word you think would make a good magnet word. The following passage is paragraph 2 of the headnote.

> Sixteen moons orbit the giant planet Jupiter. Scientists once assumed that Jupiter's moons were all rock. In the late 1970s, data from the *Voyager* spacecraft suggested something different. Images of one moon, Europa, showed chains of curving cracks called <u>cycloids</u>. These cracks usually do not appear in rock. *Galileo*, which reached Jupiter in 1995, helped solve this mystery by making three amazing discoveries.

With input from students, choose a magnet word for the passage and then choose details that relate to the word. Students may find it helpful to see the word, underlined or in capital letters, written on the board and surrounded by supporting details. For the excerpt from the MiniRead presented above, you might choose the following magnet word and supporting details.

Magnet word: mystery

Supporting details: 16 moons of Jupiter
all rock
Europa has cycloids (curving cracks)
rocks usually don't have curving cracks

Students can then create a summary sentence, using the magnet word to express the central idea. A possible summary sentence might read, "Scientists thought Jupiter's sixteen moons were all rock, but the moon Europa was a mystery because it

Reading an Informative Article *(continued)*

has cycloids, or curving cracks, which do not normally occur in rocks."

Students may also suggest *cycloids* as a magnet word because it appears underlined in the text. This would be a good opportunity to point out the significance of underlined words in an informative article. You could also create a second summary sentence, using *cycloids* as the magnet word, to illustrate the flexibility of choices of magnet words.

Applying the Strategy

Students should work in small groups to complete the worksheet, then take turns presenting their final summaries to the class. Encourage students to discuss the reasons for their choices of magnet words and the changes they made as they wrote their summaries. Students may need to use scrap paper or 3" x 5" cards to work on their summary sentences and the final summary before recording them on the worksheet.

Extending the Strategy

You may want to have students

- discuss how the strategy helped them summarize
- discuss how textbook features in the MiniRead helped them organize information
- apply the strategy to other types of texts, such as newspaper articles
- apply the strategy to the Reading Selection in the Pupil's Edition

STRATEGY OPTIONS

Some students may benefit from a discussion of the meaning of *summarizing* before they start completing the worksheet. Remind students that a summary is different from a paraphrase in that a summary includes only the main ideas of a text.

If students have trouble finding supporting details for some of their magnet words, they may need to go back and choose different magnet words.

You may wish to remind students who automatically choose underlined words as magnet words to give specific reasons for their choices.

Subtitles and headings often give clues to the reader who wants to summarize an informative article. Remind students to refer to these textbook features as they write their final summaries.

News from *Galileo*

DIRECTIONS Write your answers to the questions in the space below.

*T*he spacecraft Galileo *sailed through darkness for six years. After traveling 470 million miles, it reached its goal: the planet Jupiter. Galileo's computers whizzed into action, gathering information to send back to Earth. Scientists soon agreed that Galileo's information was worth the wait.*

Sixteen moons orbit the giant planet Jupiter. Scientists once assumed that Jupiter's moons were all rock. In the late 1970s, data from the Voyager *spacecraft suggested something different. Images of one moon, Europa, showed chains of curving cracks called* <u>cycloids</u>*. These cracks usually do not appear in rock.* Galileo, *which reached Jupiter in 1995, helped solve this mystery by making three amazing discoveries.*

> **1.** What mystery about Europa did the information from *Galileo* help to explain?

First Discovery
Water

Europa is one of the largest moons around Jupiter; it is about the size of Earth's moon. Unlike Earth's moon, Europa is covered by a three-mile-thick crust of ice. Data from *Galileo* suggests that beneath this blanket of ice, there is a sea that might be as deep as ninety miles. If this is true, Europa has twenty times more water than all the Earth's oceans put together. Scientists have not discovered large amounts of liquid water anywhere else in our <u>solar system</u>, apart from Earth. Therefore, scientists think that finding water on Europa is an important discovery.

> **2.** According to this paragraph, why is the discovery of water on Europa important?

Second Discovery
Heat

> **3.** Why are the words "gravity" and "tides" underlined in this paragraph?

The outer reaches of the solar system are extremely cold. As a result, ice is fairly common among the outermost planets—Jupiter, Saturn, Uranus, Neptune, and Pluto. None of these planets, including Jupiter, has the heat necessary to melt ice. On Europa, though, the strong pull of Jupiter's <u>gravity</u> creates 100-foot

---

cycloids *Cycloid* is a mathematical term that refers to the arc or curve of a circle.
solar system Our *solar system* consists of the sun and all the planets that circle it.
gravity *Gravity* is the force of attraction that exists between objects because of their *mass*, which is the amount of matter they are made of. Because of Jupiter's large mass, its gravity pulls powerfully on objects that are near it.

tides under the icy crust. As Europa circles Jupiter, the motion of these huge tides creates heat. Scientists think that Europa's tides make enough heat to keep its sea of water melted. Images of Europa sent back from *Galileo* support this idea. Europa's surface looks blue, white, and cracked, like a shell of ice over moving water.

Third Discovery
Organic Compounds

Other surprising things besides water and heat show up on Europa. Images from *Galileo* reveal brown smudges on Europa's crust. Scientists think the smudges are *organic compounds*—substances that contain carbon—rising from the liquid sea to stain the ice. These

compounds may have come from *mete-orites,* which are solid lumps of metal or stone that fall from space. Whatever their source, these compounds would

> **4.** In your own words, what are the main details in this paragraph?

be one key part of an important trio. Liquid water, heat, and organic compounds are the three building blocks of life. Until now, scientists believed that the only place in the solar system that contained all three elements was Earth. It is possible some form of life, perhaps single-celled plants or animals, may exist on Europa.

The good news is that scientists at the National Aeronautics and Space Administration (NASA) plan another mission that will focus only on Europa. It could provide information that will explain all of Europa's mysteries.

tides   *Tides* are the regular rise and fall of water pulled by the gravity of a sun, moon, or planet.
carbon   *Carbon* is a chemical element found in all organic compounds. It can be found in plant and animal tissues, sugars, and proteins.

Magnet Summaries

DIRECTIONS Use these steps to help you summarize the MiniRead, "News from *Galileo*."

> **STEP 1:**
> After you have read the MiniRead, talk with your group and decide which words from "News from *Galileo*" are the best magnet words, or words that are central to the article's meaning. Fill in the "cards" below and on the next page by writing one of your magnet words in the center of each one. Then, fill in each card with supporting details from the MiniRead that are related to each magnet word.

1

2

3

4

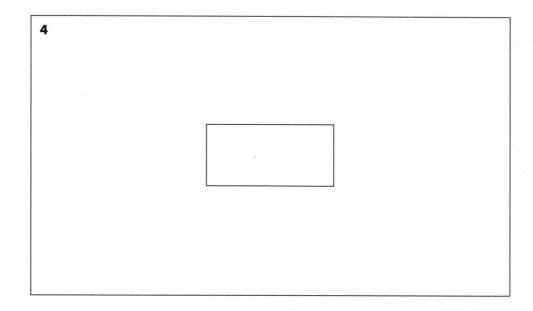

▶ **STEP 2:**

For each card, create a one-sentence summary that includes the magnet word and its most important details listed for each magnet word. (You may write two sentences if needed.) Then, in the last space below, arrange your four summary sentences to create a summary of "News from *Galileo*." You will probably need to make slight changes in each sentence when you combine it with the others, so that the paragraph will read smoothly.

Summary for Card #1:

Summary for Card #2:

Summary for Card #3:

Summary for Card #4:

Summary of "News from *Galileo*":

Reading a Persuasive Article

Pupil's Edition, page 202

Reading Skill

Point of View

Reading Focus

Logical Support

Overview

To understand persuasive texts, a reader must be able to identify the writer's point of view and analyze how well the writer supports his or her opinions. Analyzing the writer's perspective and weighing arguments can be difficult for students who lack skill in thinking critically. To comprehend and evaluate persuasive texts successfuly, students must be able to distinguish logical support from emotional appeals.

This lesson includes

- a persuasive **MiniRead,** including **Active-Reading Questions** (page 39)
- an **Alternative Strategy** for teaching persuasive texts to struggling readers (page 38)
- an **Alternative Strategy Practice** worksheet for students to apply the strategy and skill to the MiniRead (page 42)

MiniRead Summary: "Vanishing Species Vanish from Zoos"

In this persuasive article, the writer discusses how some zoos overbreed endangered species to increase their numbers. Then, to handle zoo overcrowding, zoos sell surplus animals to game dealers. Dealers in turn may sell the animals to hunting ranches. The writer's point of view is that new laws and monitoring systems are needed to prevent these abuses. The writer uses a variety of logical support to argue in favor of laws that limit breeding and prohibit the sale of zoo animals to hunting ranches. The writer also advocates setting up a national tracking system to ensure the welfare of sold animals.

Using the MiniRead

BEFORE READING Students can preview the MiniRead by looking at the title and illustrations, scanning the text, and considering what they already know about the topic. Have they visited zoos and seen signs that describe animals as "vanishing" or "endangered"? What thoughts do they have about the purpose of a zoo?

USING THE MINIREAD WITH THE PUPIL'S EDITION

After students have read and discussed the MiniRead, they may be better prepared to read the Reading Selection,"A Veto on Video Games," in the Pupil's Edition. If the MiniRead is taught in place of the Reading Selection, students will still be able to complete the Mini-Lessons and Writing Workshop.

DURING READING Students may want to work in pairs to read and answer the questions or take turns reading portions of the MiniRead aloud before they answer each question. They can write their responses in the margins of the MiniRead.

AFTER READING Students can complete the **Alternative Strategy Practice** worksheet on their own before discussing their responses in small groups.

Reading a Persuasive Article *(continued)*

Save the Last Word for Me

To use this strategy, students read a text, choose the part that they think best sums up the writer's point of view, and write their reasons for choosing it. Each student then reads his or her chosen passage to other students in a small group. Group members take turns commenting on the passage. Then, the student who chose the passage gets the last word in the discussion by explaining the reasons for his or her choice. At this point, the other students are not allowed to respond.

Modeling the Strategy

After students have read the MiniRead, choose a passage that you consider persuasive and read it aloud. For instance, you might choose the second paragraph of the MiniRead. Students then comment on the point of view expressed in the passage. Comments might include, "Maybe selling zoo animals is illegal, since the dealers are selling them without the zoos' knowledge," or "Anyone who cares enough about animals to have a zoo shouldn't sell animals to hunting ranches."

To explain why you chose this passage, you might say that it illustrates the fact that zoos sometimes sell animals to irresponsible people. You may want to ask students what the passage reveals about the writer's point of view and what logical and emotional appeals the writer uses in the passage.

STRATEGY OPTIONS

You may wish to discuss examples of logical appeals with students before they apply the strategy.

If students have trouble identifying the writer's point of view in their chosen passages, they may need to go back and choose a different passage.

Students can do an analysis of logical and emotional appeals in the MiniRead by mapping out the writer's point of view, reasons, and evidence, as shown in the Pupil's Edition, page 208.

Applying the Strategy

Students should complete the worksheet, then take turns sharing and responding in small groups. Students may have chosen different passages, but there is not a right or wrong answer in this exercise. It is important for each group to allow the student who chose the passage to have the last word in the discussion.

Extending the Strategy

You may want to have students

- discuss how the strategy helped them identify the writer's point of view
- apply the strategy to the Reading Selection in the Pupil's Edition
- apply the strategy to other types of texts, such as editorials, campaign speeches, and letters to the editor

Vanishing Species Vanish from Zoos

Mini Read

DIRECTIONS Write your answers to the questions in the space below.

Are you up to your armpits in antelopes or rolling in reptiles? The answer is yes for many zoos in the United States. Zoo overcrowding has become a big problem. Many zoos work to save animal species that have almost disappeared in the wild by breeding them to increase their numbers.

> **1.** What issue is described here?

Breeding programs have been so successful, though, that some zoos now have too many of these endangered animals and not enough space for them. To handle this problem, most zoos sell their extra animals to other zoos.

While most of the sales are to other zoos, unfortunately, some are to game dealers. A dealer may then sell the animals at auctions. Some animals are bought by collectors who might not know how to care for them. Others are bought by people who own hunting ranches. At these ranches, customers pay a lot of money to hunt captive animals. Most zoo animals have become so tame they do not even try to escape during a hunt.

It may come as a surprise that selling zoo animals for these purposes is legal. A zoo's main responsibility should be to preserve and protect wildlife. To help zoos achieve that goal, laws should be passed to protect animals that zoos must sell.

> **2.** What is the writer's opinion about the sale of zoo animals?

First, there should be laws against selling animals to hunting ranches. The American Zoo and Aquarium Association is a group of zoos that has established strict rules for the treatment of zoo animals. It forbids zoos to sell animals to "roadside zoos, hunting ranches, pet traders, or livestock auctions." In reality the Association has no legal power to make zoos follow these rules. The Humane Society of the United States says that many zoos just ignore these rules. After a three-year investigation, the Humane Society charged forty zoos with selling animals to hunting ranches, either directly or through dealers. The Society backed up its charges with evidence from the Texas Animal Health Commission, which keeps track of all exotic animals brought into Texas.

> **3.** What facts does the writer present in this paragraph to support the need for new laws?

The Association admits that it cannot keep track of all the animals sold by zoos. Clearly, we need a national system to record and check up on these sales, including background checks on people who buy. In 1999, for instance, a zookeeper pleaded guilty to selling endangered Australian pythons to a game dealer for $70,000. The zoo's spokesperson said the keeper did this without the zoo's knowledge. A lawyer involved with the case said that, in her opinion, the zookeeper probably thought no one would care because the reptiles were not cute, cuddly creatures.

> **4.** Why does the writer include the story about the zookeeper?

Finally, it should be against the law for zoos to produce more animals than they can care for. Breeding animals in captivity is neces-

Vanishing Species Vanish from Zoos *(continued)*

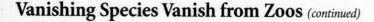

5. What is the main point of this paragraph? Why does the writer include the opinions of Asis and Landres?

sary for the survival of endangered species, but zoos also need to prevent overcrowding and selling to dealers. Karen Asis, an Association spokesperson, advises, "Instead of merely . . . breeding animals, zoos must begin to take measures to control reproduction." Lisa Landres of a group called Friends of Animals agrees. She says that zoos should not breed animals unless they can provide lifetime care for them.

Every zoo animal is at our mercy. How can we allow species endangered in the wild to be threatened in the zoo, also? A system must be established to keep track of each and every sold animal, so they never fall into the hands of people who might harm or neglect them. Laws must be passed and enforced to limit breeding and to prevent zoo animals from ending up at hunting ranches. Thanks to our nation's zoos, future generations should be able to see and appreciate the amazing wildlife who share our planet. Unless lawmakers take action to guarantee the life and safety of endangered species, this valuable legacy is in danger of vanishing.

6. What, if anything, in this paragraph convinces you to accept the writer's opinion?

Save the Last Word for Me

DIRECTIONS Use these steps to apply the **Save the Last Word for Me** strategy to the MiniRead, "Vanishing Species Vanish from Zoos."

STEP 1:
Choose the passage from the MiniRead that you think is the most persuasive. Circle the passage. It may be a single sentence or a whole paragraph or more.

STEP 2:
Use the graphic organizer below to help you analyze why the passage you chose is persuasive.

This passage is persuasive because …

How the passage appeals to my feelings:

How the passage influences my thoughts:

How the passage reveals the writer's purpose and point of view:

Reading a Print Advertisement
Pupil's Edition, page 234

Reading Skill

Making Inferences: Forming Generalizations

Reading Focus

Persuasive Techniques

Overview

The goal of advertising is to persuade people to make positive generalizations that will lead them to buy a product or service. To evaluate a print ad, readers must be able to form generalizations about the ad and then decide whether they agree or disagree with what the ad suggests. Some readers have trouble analyzing information in a wider context and then making generalizations. They are unable to connect what they read with what they already know to make an inference that applies to the general world.

This lesson includes

- a print advertisement **MiniRead,** including **Active-Reading Questions** (page 46)
- an **Alternative Strategy** for teaching print advertisements to struggling readers (page 44)
- an **Alternative Strategy Practice** worksheet for students to apply the strategy and skill to the MiniRead (page 47)

MiniRead Summary: "If You Really Care About Your Family . . ."

This print advertisement uses persuasive techniques to suggest a potentially dangerous situation in which safety may depend on having a cellphone. The ad shows a broken-down car in the snow and says "Your kids are scared and freezing." The text of the ad targets the reader's fear of this situation as well as the reader's sense of responsibility to take preventative measures. The purpose of the ad is to persuade the reader to subscribe to "Super CellPhone SOS" for $39.95 a month.

Using the MiniRead

BEFORE READING Students may preview the advertisement by reading the opening slogan and glancing at the images. Do they or people they know have cellphones? What are some reasons people keep phones in their cars?

DURING READING Students may want to work in pairs to read and answer the questions or take turns reading portions of the MiniRead aloud before they answer each question. They can write their responses in the margins of the MiniRead.

AFTER READING Students can complete the **Alternative Strategy Practice** worksheet alone or in pairs. Then, they can share their responses with the class.

USING THE MINIREAD WITH THE PUPIL'S EDITION

After students have read and discussed the MiniRead, they may be better prepared to read the Reading Selection, "Leukemia Made Him a Patient; We Helped Him Become a Kid Again," in the Pupil's Edition. If the MiniRead is taught in place of the Reading Selection, students will still be able to complete the Mini-Lessons and Writing Workshop.

Reading a Print Advertisement *(continued)*

It Says . . . I Say

To use this strategy, students complete a chart that guides them through making inferences to answer questions about a text. First they find information in the text that addresses a question and record it in the *It Says* column of the chart. Next, they record their thoughts about that information in the *I Say* column. Then, in the *And So* column, they combine the textual support with their own personal response to make an inference. From that inference, they then make a generalization in the *My Generalization* column of the chart.

Modeling the Strategy

After students have read the MiniRead, show them an It Says . . . I Say chart like the one below that contains the question shown in column 1.

Question	It Says (What the text says)	I Say (My response)	And So (My answer)	My Generalization
What does the ad suggest these parents should have done?				

Ask students to look at the advertisement and find information that relates to the question. Fill in the chart as a class, writing information from the text under the *It Says* column. Possible responses include, "They don't have any way of calling for help," "They're getting colder every minute," and, "There's nothing they can do but howl at the moon." Then, ask students to offer their reactions to the ad in the *I Say* column. Responses may include, "I'd always have my cellphone with me," "I would have had my car checked before I went on the trip," or, "I would try to flag down another driver, if one came." Students may discuss and debate their responses.

Students should then try to use the text and their own thoughts to create an inference for the *And So* column. An inference may be, "The ad is suggesting that the parents should have prepared for this emergency by getting a cellphone." Next, discuss with students possible generalizations they could make from their inferences. One generalization might be, "People should take safety precautions, like carrying a cellphone, in case an emergency arises."

Reading a Print Advertisement *(continued)*

You may want to have a discussion of persuasive techniques the advertisement uses. What is the advertiser's goal? Do students feel that their emotions are being manipulated? Would they buy the cellphone service after reading an ad like this? Why or why not?

Applying the Strategy

Students should complete the worksheet, then take turns sharing and responding in small groups. Students may have several comments per question in the *It Says* and *I Say* columns, but they should have only one answer per question in the *And So* and *My Generalization* columns. Some students may need to be told how many *It Says* comments to list. Since each person's prior knowledge and perspective is different, students should understand that the generalizations they make will vary.

Extending the Strategy

You may want to have students

- discuss how the strategy helped them make generalizations about an advertisement and analyze the persuasiveness of its message
- apply the strategy to the Reading Selection in the Pupil's Edition
- apply the strategy to other advertisements, such as billboards, TV advertisements, and radio advertisements

Print Advertisement

DIRECTIONS Write your answers to the questions in the space below.

If You Really Care About Your Family . . . Be Prepared with Super CellPhone SOS

1. What emotions or thoughts do you have after reading the ad's opening slogan and first sentence?

You are traveling down a deserted back road at midnight in the dead of winter. Suddenly, your car breaks down.

Your kids are scared and freezing. Now what do you do—consult the owner's manual or howl at the moon?

If you have **SUPER CELLPHONE SOS,** all you need to do is call our 24-hour emergency hot line.

2. Why does the ad directly address the reader, repeating the word "you"?

With **SUPER CELLPHONE SOS,** help is always just a phone call away. When you call our hot line, we will pinpoint your location immediately and send help to you <u>anywhere</u> in the United States.

If you care about your family, you can't afford to be without **SUPER CELLPHONE SOS.** For just $39.95 a month, you can breathe a sigh of relief, knowing your family will always be safe on the road.

3. What does the ad suggest might happen if you do not sign up for this service?

To find a **SUPER CELLPHONE** dealer near you, just call 1-800-555-2626. You'll be glad you did.

4. Who are the advertisers trying to persuade? Is the ad convincing? Explain.

It Says . . . I Say

DIRECTIONS Use these steps to apply the **It Says . . . I Say** strategy to the MiniRead, "If You Really Care About Your Family . . ."

- Read the MiniRead. Then read the questions in column 1 of the chart below.
- Answer the first question by finding information in the text that relates to the question. Record that information in the **It Says** column. Use direct quotations from the text.
- In the **I Say** column, write your own response to the question. Explain what the information from the text means to you.
- Combine the information in the **It Says** column with your comments in the **I Say** column to answer the question. Write your answer in the **And So** column.
- Based on your answer, make a generalization connected to the question and write it in the **My Generalization** column.
- Follow the same steps for questions 2 and 3.

Question	It Says (What the text says)	I Say (My response)	And So (My answer)	My Generalization
1. What emotional effects is the ad trying to create in the reader?				
2. What does the advertisement imply about people who do not subscribe to Super Cell-Phone SOS?				

▶ Question	▶ It Says (What the text says)	▶ I Say (My response)	▶ And So (My answer)	▶ My Generalization
3. According to the advertisement, what does the Super Cell-Phone SOS customer receive besides cell-phone service and an emergency hot line?				

Answer Key

Chapter 1

"Going . . . Going . . . Gone!"

p. 4 | Active-Reading Questions

Answers will vary. Sample responses follow.

1. The writer uses specific images, such as "ballpark hot dogs," "flashing colors on the giant message boards," and "booming music on the loudspeakers." The phrase "electricity in the air" conveys the excitement of the crowd.

2. I think the essay will be about which player—Sammy Sosa or Mark McGwire—breaks the home-run record.

3. The mood is one of suspense and anticipation.

4. The writer says that the fans acted almost as one person: "Fifty thousand fans seemed to jump to their feet all at once" and "everyone in the stadium seemed to lean forward together to watch the ball." Other details are "earsplitting cheers," "thousands of red Cardinal jerseys," "joyful smiles," and flashing cameras. The details create a feeling of energy, excitement, and suspense.

5. The writer probably wanted to show Sosa's generosity, good sportsmanship, and real friendship.

6. The game was important because a record was broken, strangers in the stands felt a camaraderie, and McGwire and Sosa were both winners in different ways.

p. 6 | Alternative Strategy Practice

Answers will vary. Sample responses follow.

Step 1

hero

Step 2

I think "hero" is the most important word because the story is about two kinds of heroism: McGwire's heroic breaking of the record and Sosa's heroic congratulating of his friend despite his own disappointment.

Step 3

Even though Mark McGwire broke the home run record in 1998, Sammy Sosa was also a hero because he was happy for his friend.

Step 4

After the discussion, I think the most important word in the MiniRead is "brothers." The most important thing about the story is that Sosa and McGwire acted like brothers. Eventually one of them was probably going to hit that home run, so the question of who would win was less important than the bond between the two players.

Chapter 2

"The Crabmaster"

p. 9 | Active-Reading Questions

Wording of answers will vary but should reflect the ideas below. Sample responses follow.

1. The writer wants to inform the reader that crab is a delicious but complicated food and wants to teach people how to eat it. The writer also seeks to entertain the reader.

2. I conclude that eating crabs is an informal, messy activity that requires a little bit of preparation.

3. Yes. The legs do not have to be eaten before the claws. But if a person is just learning how to eat a crab, he or she is probably better off beginning with the legs because they are easier to eat.

4. Turn the claw in its socket to detach it from the body. Open it by cracking it with a nutcracker, or by placing a knife over it and driving the knife through the shell with a mallet. Or you can just smash the shell and pick any shell fragments off the meat.

5. The writer describes the "tab" by which you can open the body, and gives examples of the parts you shouldn't eat such as intestines and gills. The writer explains that you should remove those parts and then eat the meat that remains in the shell.

p. 12 | Alternative Strategy Practice

Responses will vary widely. Students should be able to support their opinions with specific evidence from the MiniRead.

Chapter 3

"To e, or Not to e"

p. 16 | Active-Reading Questions

Wording of answers will vary but should reflect the ideas below. Sample responses follow.

1. The writer is going to discuss the advantages and disadvantages of using e-mail.

2. The main advantages e-mail shares with letters are the chance to revise before sending and the ability of the recipient to re-read the message as many times as he or she wishes. E-mail is better than letters in that corrections are easier to make, and you can attach copies of previous e-mails or of other documents without photocopying or paying extra postage.

3. I think e-mail is better than a phone call. It's fast, doesn't interrupt the recipient, and gives people a record of their conversations. Also, if you need to send the same message to lots of people, e-mail is much faster than phone calls.

4. It discusses disadvantages. I can tell from the section heading and from the first sentence, "The bad side of e-mail is that sometimes it simply does not work."

5. I think e-mail is better than letters or telephone calls for some types of communication, such as business memos or brief notes to friends. For other types of communication, though, letters or phone calls are more appropriate. I think every form of communication has its own advantages and disadvantages, so we need to choose the one that is appropriate to our situation.

p. 19 | Alternative Strategy Practice

Sketches, explanations, and conclusions will vary widely. Students should be able to support their

conclusions with specific evidence from the MiniRead.

Chapter 4

"Julie of the Wolves Book Jacket"

p. 24 | Active-Reading Questions

Wording of answers will vary but should reflect the ideas below. Sample responses follow.

1. The title mentions the name "Julie" and the illustration shows a family of wolves, so I think the book will be about a girl living with wolves.

2. The phrases suggest that this book is going to contain exciting action as well as a story about emotions.

3. Julie's problems include the loss of her parents, her disagreement with the old ways of the elders, getting lost in the Alaskan wilderness, and having to choose whether to live among wolves or people. These are challenging problems to face. I would like to know how she solves them.

4. Yes. The paragraph says that she grew up learning about wild animals on her family's farm. Also, she studied the behavior of wolves in Alaska.

5. While in Alaska studying wolves, Jean George thought of the idea for the book. After seeing a young Inuit girl walking into the wilderness by herself, she envisioned the character of Julie.

6. They both love wolves and nature, and they both like to teach others about nature.

p. 28 | Alternative Strategy Practice

Comments and tallies will vary widely. Students should try to make different types of comments as noted on the worksheet.

Chapter 5

"News from *Galileo*"

p. 32 | Active-Reading Questions

Wording of answers will vary but should reflect the ideas below. Sample responses follow.

1. It helped to explain why Europa had curving cracks (cycloids), which indicated that Europa might not be rock.

2. It's important because large amounts of liquid water have not been found anywhere else in the solar system, except on Earth.

3. They are underlined to call the reader's attention to the fact that they are defined at the bottom of the page.

4. The main details are that Europa has brown smudges on its crust (which might represent the presence of organic compounds) and that the presence of liquid water, heat, and organic compounds on Europa may indicate that it has life forms.

p. 34 | Alternative Strategy Practice

Answers will vary. Sample responses follow.

Step 1

Magnet Word #1:	*Galileo*
Supporting Details:	reached Jupiter in 1995
	moon Europa
	cycloids
	three discoveries
Magnet Word #2:	water
Supporting Details:	Europa has ice crust
	sea underneath
	20 times Earth's water
	large amounts of liquid
	water nowhere
	else in solar system
	(except Earth)
Magnet Word #3:	heat
Supporting Details:	no planet has enough
	heat to melt ice
	Jupiter's gravity
	Europa has tides
	tides create heat

Magnet Word #4:	organic compounds
Supporting Details:	carbon
	liquid water and heat
	building blocks of life
	form of life

Step 2

Summary for Card #1: In 1995, when the spacecraft *Galileo* reached Jupiter and its moon Europa, which contains cycloids, it made three discoveries that suggested that Europa was not just rock.

Summary for Card #2: Under Europa's crust of ice, *Galileo* discovered 20 times the amount of liquid water found on Earth; this is the only place in the solar system other than Earth where so much liquid water has been found.

Summary for Card #3: Unlike the outer planets, Europa has enough heat to melt ice; this heat is probably created by the movement of tides caused by Jupiter's gravity acting on Europa.

Summary for Card #4: Europa might have organic compounds made of carbon which, together with liquid water and heat, make up the building blocks of life; therefore, it's possible some form of life exists on Europa.

Summary of "News from *Galileo*": The spacecraft *Galileo* reached Jupiter in 1995 and made three discoveries about the moon Europa, which was already unusual because it had cycloids (curving cracks). The discoveries suggested that Europa was not just rock. The first discovery was that Europa has liquid water under its crust of ice—in fact, 20 times the amount of water on Earth. This is significant because large amounts of liquid water are found nowhere else in the solar system except on Earth. The second discovery is that unlike the outer planets, Europa has enough heat to melt ice; the heat is probably created by the movement of tides. Finally, *Galileo* discovered that Europa might have organic compounds (those containing carbon), which, together with liquid water and heat, make up the conditions for creating life. These three discoveries indicate that there could be life on Europa.

Answer Key (cont.)

Chapter 6

"Vanishing Species Vanish from Zoos"

p. 39 | Active-Reading Questions

The wording of answers to questions 1–5 will vary but should reflect the ideas below. Sample responses follow.

1. The issue is the overcrowding of zoos due to the overbreeding of zoo animals.

2. The writer thinks that the sale of zoo animals should be regulated by laws.

3. The writer points out that the American Zoo and Aquarium Association, which tries to govern the sale of animals, has no power to enforce its rules and that some zoos simply ignore the rules.

4. The story illustrates the need for a system to record and track the sale of zoo animals.

5. The point is that it should be illegal for zoos to breed more animals than they can care for themselves. Asis and Landres are quoted to show that spokespeople from organizations that protect animals share the author's opinion.

6. Sample answer: The sentence "Every zoo animal is at our mercy" wins me over. If animals are our captives, then we are responsible for the way they are treated. I think we have a responsibility to pass laws to limit breeding and prevent this unnecessary cruelty.

p. 42 Alternative Strategy Practice

Answers will vary. Sample responses follow.

Step 1

Passage:

"The Association admits that it cannot keep track of all the animals sold by zoos. Clearly, we need a national system to record and check up on these sales, including background checks on people who buy. In 1999, for instance, a zookeeper pleaded guilty to selling endangered Australian pythons to a game dealer for $70,000."

Step 2

This passage is persuasive because . . .
The passage shows that some of the people entrusted with zoo animals may let animals be abused in order to make a profit.

How the passage appeals to my feelings: It made me really mad that a zookeeper didn't care what happened to the Australian pythons as long as he made money from their sale.

How the passage influences my thoughts: It makes me think there should be better regulation of zoos.

How the passage reveals the writer's purpose and point of view: By giving an example of how people illegally sell endangered zoo animals, the writer reveals and reinforces his purpose: to persuade people that laws should be passed to regulate the sale of these animals. The phrases "The Association *admits* . . ." and "*Clearly,* we need a national system . . ." also reveal the writer's point of view that regulating the sale of zoo animals is a necessity and a matter of urgency.

Chapter 7

"If You Really Care About Your Family . . ."

p. 46 | Active-Reading Questions

Answers will vary but should indicate that students have read the text. Sample responses follow.

1. These sentences make me worry about the possibility that my family could get stuck in the middle of nowhere in cold weather.

2. The ad wants the reader to take the message personally and think of his or her own family in an emergency.

3. The ad suggests that if you do not sign up for the service, your family might be in an unsafe situation in the future without any way to get help.

4. The advertisers are trying to persuade anyone who has a family. I think the ad is convincing because people have a strong desire to protect their families from possible danger.

p. 47 | Alternative Strategy Practice

Answers will vary but should reflect a thoughtful response to the text. Sample responses follow.

1. **What emotional effects is the ad trying to create in the reader?**

It Says: The ad uses phrases like "deserted back road," "dead of winter," and "freezing."

I Say: I would not want to be stuck in a broken-down car in the middle of nowhere in winter. I would wonder how I could get help and worry about my safety.

And So: The writer is trying to create fear in the reader of being stuck in a dangerous, helpless situation.

My Generalization: One of the ways advertisers sell products is by creating fear or anxiety in the reader, then assuring the reader that the product will protect them from a threat.

2. **What does the advertisement imply about people who do not subscribe to Super CellPhone SOS?**

It Says: The ad uses the phrases "If you care about your family," and "your family will always be safe on the road."

I Say: The next person who drives by might not help. They might even try to rob the family. Or maybe nobody will drive by for hours.

There may not be a telephone nearby. People who care about their families will do what they can to avoid this situation.

And So: The advertisement is trying to say that people who won't spend the $39.95 a month don't care about their families.

My Generalization: Another strategy advertisers use is to try to make people feel guilty, for instance, if they don't buy the product, they don't care about their families.

3. **According to the advertisement, what does the Super CellPhone SOS customer receive besides cellphone service and an emergency hotline?**

It Says: The ad uses the phrases "you can breathe a sigh of relief" and "you'll be glad you did."

I Say: When I breathe a sigh of relief, it's because I feel that I have escaped something bad that I thought was going to happen to me.

And So: The advertisement promises peace of mind.

My Generalization: Advertisers like to make readers think that the product will bring them something greater than a service or item, like happiness or peace of mind.